American Folk Songs for Two

10 American Folk Songs Arranged for Two Voices and Piano
For Recitals, Concerts, and Contests

COMPILED AND EDITED BY ANDY BECK

Table of Contents

Sally K. Albrecht, Piano • Kent Heckman, Engineer
Piano accompaniments were recorded at Red Rock Recording in Saylorsburg, PA.

Cover Art: Country Twins, 2011
By Debbie "Mama" Criswell (b.1967)
Acrylic on canvas (16" by 12")
From the collection of Jay Althouse and Sally K. Albrecht

Debbie "Mama" Criswell is a self-taught artist, currently living in Clinton, Tennessee. She is the single mother of two girls and a boy, and has been a professional artist since 2003. She was inspired by the rolling hills, tall farm houses, and Amish families she observed while living in a small Missouri town. Debbie is primarily known for the primitive folk style of her paintings, but also dabbles in abstracts. Her works have been sold throughout the world, and are currently available on eBay and in galleries throughout the United States.

Book (00-38106)   ISBN-10: 0-7390-8869-6   ISBN-13: 978-0-7390-8869-2
Accompaniment CD (00-38107)   ISBN-10: 0-7390-8870-X   ISBN-13: 978-0-7390-8870-8
Book & CD (00-38108)   ISBN-10: 0-7390-8871-8   ISBN-13: 978-0-7390-8871-5

The solos in this collection were adapted from Alfred choral arrangements.
Please visit **alfred.com** or contact your favorite music dealer for more information.

Billy Boy
Arranged by Mark Hayes
SATB (21198)
SAB (21199)

Down in the Valley to Pray
Arranged by Jay Althouse
SATB (23637)
SAB (23638)

Every Night When the Sun Goes In
Arranged by David Waggoner
SATB (37926)
SAB (37927)
2-Part (37928)

Go 'Way from My Window
Arranged by Ruth Elaine Schram
SATB (16338)
SAB/3-Part Mixed (16339)
SSA (16335)

How Can I Keep from Singing?
Arranged by Andy Beck
SATB (28576)
SAB (28577)
SSA (28578)

Poor Boy
Arranged by Ruth Elaine Schram
SSA (31079)

Simple Gifts
Arranged by Andy Beck
SATB (27074)
SAB (27075)
2-Part (27076)

Sourwood Mountain
Arranged by Ruth Elaine Schram
SATB (SVM05023)
3-Part Mixed (SVM05024)
2-Part (SVM05025)
TBB (SVM05026)

Sun Don't Set in the Mornin'
Arranged by Jay Althouse
SATB (24031)
SAB (24032)
SSA (24033)

The Water Is Wide
Arranged by Mark Hayes
SATB (20187)
SAB (20188)
SSA (20189)

1. BILLY BOY

American Folk Song
Arranged by **MARK HAYES**

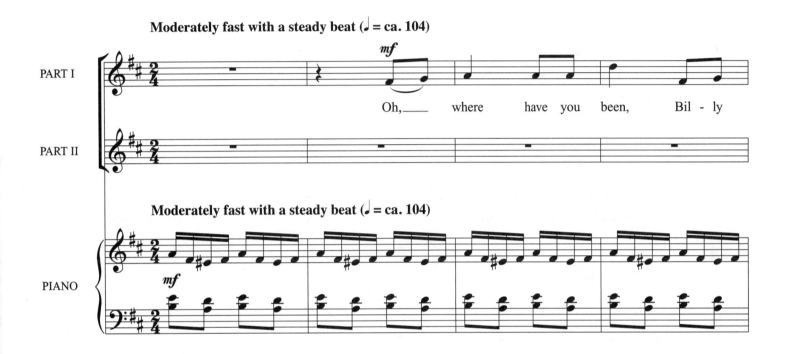

young thing and can-not leave her moth - er._____

Did she set you a chair, Bil - ly

Did she set you a chair, Bil - ly

2. DOWN IN THE VALLEY TO PRAY

Southern Folk Ballad
Arranged by **JAY ALTHOUSE**

3. EVERY NIGHT WHEN THE SUN GOES IN

Appalachian Folk Song
Arranged by **DAVID WAGGONER**

4. GO 'WAY FROM MY WINDOW

American Folk Song
Arranged by **RUTH ELAINE SCHRAM**

38106

5. HOW CAN I KEEP FROM SINGING?

American Folk Hymn
Arranged by **ANDY BECK**

30

38106

6. POOR BOY

American Folk Song
Arranged by **RUTH ELAINE SCHRAM**

7. SIMPLE GIFTS

American Shaker Song
Arranged by **ANDY BECK**

15

when we find our-selves in the place just right, 'twill be in the val - ley of love and de-

19
mp
When true sim-plic - i - ty is gained, to bow and to bend we shan't be a-shamed.___

light._____

23

___ To turn, turn will be our de-light, 'till by turn - ing, turn - ing we

mp
To turn, turn will be our de-light, 'till by turn - ing, turn - ing we

42

8. SOURWOOD MOUNTAIN

Appalachian Folk Song
Arranged by **RUTH ELAINE SCHRAM**

Lyrics:

So man-y girls I just can't count 'em, so man-y girls on Sour-wood Moun-tain,

So man-y girls I just can't count 'em, so man-y girls on Sour-wood Moun-tain,

so man-y girls. Hey! Hey, dee-dle dum day.

hey, hey on Sour-wood Moun-tain. Hey! Hey, dee-dle dum day.

50

38106

9. SUN DON'T SET IN THE MORNIN'

Traditional Words
with new verses by **JAY ALTHOUSE**

Based on a Southern Folk Hymn
Adapted and Arranged by
JAY ALTHOUSE

38106

10. THE WATER IS WIDE

American Folk Song
Arranged by **MARK HAYES**

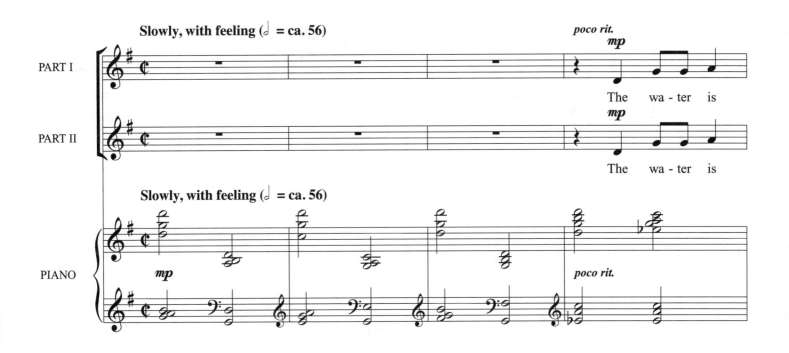